TIME DOWN TO MIND

GRAHAM FOUST

TIME
DOWN
TO
MIND

Flood Editions

Chicago

There is the tarnish; and there, the imperishable wish.

MARIANNE MOORE

TIME DOWN TO MIND

CONCEPTUAL POEM

I love a map for its inaccuracies,
a certain pearl for its certain pearl-ness.
I wouldn't hurt a fly, but I'd kill one,

a way of life that keeps me asleep nights,
as if adrift in a niche of big oil.
Symmetry is more or less more

and less bunk—another hole, another
doily; the phrase "be that as it may";
the fucking Milky Way by any other name . . .

A touch horrific is the green with which
the ground will tear the winter. I write this
as a florist muscles daisies into place.

FOUND POEM

We force into meanings that don't concern us:

cords of wood stacked all over the neighborhood;
articles left with ex-lovers; the famous;
and always the Interstate out there, like surf.

There is no point in speaking or not speaking.
There is only a crow in a tree—make notes.

I have a wanderer's sadness at evening,

father, and further—the migration of things!—
not much grows here anymore, except bodies
below the softening shales, bereft of you,

and this (forgive me) is like carrying coals.
It's winter, it's after supper, it's goodbye—

many of the images refuse to part.

Gesticulation—it is half the language,
the coming back from going where and touching.
Don't you remember how free the future seemed?

Think fast! (Still dreaming?) The boy had caught his friend.
The keyboard gone in the rank grass swept her hand.

Wanted, fought toward, dreamed of, all a green living,

each leaf would seem to require its own quatrain—
carelessly nailed, looking like nothing at all—
and the road twisted on to his loveless house.

Does the dust of it rise to meet you, mornings,
the only conquered evening darlinged away?

NINETEEN EIGHTY-THREE

Most of my parents' friends seemed dumber than mine.
One of them, Joe, had a license plate stolen,
and one day while jogging he happened upon
some other poor jerk's plate lying in the road.
Ecstatic that it shared two letters with his,
he ran home with it and used some gaffer's tape
to change a black number seven to an eight,
et cetera. This in fact fooled nobody.

Not a week later, the cops pulled him over,
fined him, informed him that they could lock him up.
He was livid, but he was also forty,
which to me meant he'd run half out of himself.
I was thirteen and couldn't shake the belief
that the world consisted mostly of police.

PREP

To let another come as far as you
with sunflowers, scissors, a Mason jar
somehow, the hot sky over everything;
the dark obligations mindfulness brings,
those bits of invasion called "your feelings"
in the event that they require a name—
anything that might be love could mean shame.
Think how power, that forever-wet wind,
seems to come by itself quite naturally;
how what happens now has happened thus far:
somebody somewhere more or less saying,
"I just called because it's my job to call
to make sure the man you said was dead is."
Daydark like a cave up here in the head,
its core a stockpile of talkative jewels,
I'm walking and trying to hold too much,
a win-lose-lose-lose-lose situation.
But what of it—what not of it, really,
when you get right down to it, which I will
before too long or shortly thereafter,
while familiars come ticking through pictures.
Mind's its own consort, logic its own whore—
gonna go on getting any younger.
All day scraping my way back to the day,
I pull myself together in a way

I wouldn't think to make a camera
or a chimera were I to have to,
though I do, and it's only the present,
so I can't know when things will cease to work,
that whiskey's cheaper just six blocks away.
The insect-like clicks of a bicycle
behind me are the sounds I'd expect
from a poem or two, and so it goes . . .
Prep for what can never be continues.

SPORT UTILITY POEM

Here's to good friends. Tonight is kinda special.
There's no fuselage like lack of enjambment.
You meant to dream a kingdom of beginnings,
but meaning comes after dreams, no matter what
some commercial for German beer might suggest.
Hamstrung by abundance, another poem
in English, official language of traffic
and other things that happen the world over,
at least according to streaming video,
the official language of streamed video
the world over insofar as you know it.
Paint a different color—maybe the color
of some meat's juices cooked clear—on your front door.
You're the king of this jungle of suffixes.

9/10/11

for Geoffrey G. O'Brien

Proximity isn't necessarily
possibility—for example, while I
could eat my teeth, I could never say them, nor
could I say rain inscribes this page, that pavement—
but here in the marked-down hum of broken meaning
can we agree on peace's casualties?
A decade of what I made of clarity:
idea causes pain that builds brains of its own.
Only numbers mean anything or nothing.
Oh! Blessèd rage for comfort, a fifth of Patrón.
And if I curse the world's useful miseries,
can I tell you, too, how fond I am of Earth
upon deboarding the redeye to New York
from San Francisco after jokes in my sleep,
as each New York minute unquietly pounds
itself out, the clouds too huge to have to count,
the horizon post-fuck-up untouchable?
That I always almost don't get what I want
makes me crazy; would make me what, upper crust
in some parts of history, but never now,
when I make rent, or way back when, when I can't.
I *can* say rain makes the pavement look supple—

a decade of what I thought was clarity:
ten short years of *that* and then actual bells.
To think to not believe I was ever here's
the cost of my living, the rickety thing.
Health might be my having only felt alive.

THE SHAPES I'M IN

Wherever there moves a human element
there follows an infinite antagony.

There's something in me clamors to not get out.

⌄

To start to breathe is beyond all sentences;
to start to bleed is beyond all rhetoric.

Tied to and tired of every idea,
I try to refresh my browser to death,
but it can't yet think to let me do that,
so I listen off the weather instead;
am become worse, of course, for lack of wear.

⌄

Overcast skies make the city night brighter.

Setting out for what's desired unbridles dread.

NIGHT YEARS

An oak leaf falls through the moonroof of the car,
as in a motion picture by whomever.

A little quiet and it all comes apart.
A little quiet and it all comes apart.

Finally asleep, my daughter's gone to me.
Earlier, biting a doll, she was right here.

LET THIS BE THE POEM FOR

A FACE I ALMOST MADE

Let this be a poem for the face I almost made.
It took forever not to heal is only surrealist if you mean it.

If there's heaven, it's an acquired science,
an announcement of the psyche to the sky's deep white

as if some clarity had somehow been arrived at overnight
so as to let me speak to how that's working out for me.

The tree's green's wet echoes shelve the wren's nest rather
    surgically,
and I have other thoughts the same green seems to soundtrack
    mock heroically

while logic's hooks tear that life into this one, little worse,
singing, "Don't you read the water; don't you ever eat the light
    that reeks of prose."

BEACH

Breeze, gull, water—none heard over another;
my rage against surplus not quite satisfied.

I live nearby, but I don't come much, do I?

I could never say I "found" grains of sand here.

JEOPARDY

Just off campus, ridiculous, precious—
a little green Bible in a puddle.

Like his or hers, mine's a promise made of swerves;
a mostly honest and dreamt-around-in knot
I find remarkable to have to undo.

This face, the safest,
much Christ of which
tonight makes little use.

Who is Graham Foust?

I'd like to think so.

Primitive half-light with positive monster,
the white flat cold of the sky skinned over,

not everything fits on this horizon's crease,
and what doesn't fit can only be called mine.

Whatever sort of story the mind might be,
whatever kind of hieroglyph the body,

I concede and love them conditionally—
as though both should last forever—all the time.

EPITHALAMIUM

It isn't Christmas, but some Christmas lights
are shaking in the wind a small fan makes.
Our teeth squeak into day-old kimmelwecks,
and we'll promise to not live differently
so help us tolerable floor glitter,
the origin of which we're unaware;
so help us cellophaned orchid, set out
as if gouged from a mountain; so help us
vanished unhappinesses, and also
any other unseen things on this porch,
the aid of which might be worth enlisting.
Almost not summer, it's warm as summer,
and our guests will soon arrive, their dull gifts.
Something's come to substitute for comfort,
and it's not our having been lost to this.

WITH TWO CHILDREN ALL DAY

That the manner of my blood comes
back to me as something
like the difference between the dead
and the imagined has me thinking:
one doesn't engineer one's perversions.

ᵕ

Want of the world's a little
like a movie in 3-D—

I paw at what's unreal;
it seems to be there.

ᵕ

That there's a drain here at the heart
of this oasis doesn't worry me.

What worries me's how very much
I love a good mirage.

Clarity is equal parts rigor and drift.
Think of a state of mind and you're not in it.

If wanting to possess causes fear of loss,
then the subject has always been vanishing.

THE BETTER PERSON

Our upstairs neighbors are moving stuff around.

Small children do a thing I call "the laugh cry."

California's sunshine's as mean as ten swans.

Most tragedies would give us up endlessly.

⌄

To make, to love, and to destroy like a voice
the spotless window of the infinitive.
And to leave the place that nurtured you afraid.

What changes, slightly, is the will not to change,
as if all language went about it all wrong.

SUPPOSED TO HAVE BEEN

WRITTEN IN AMERICA

There's a flag in the notion
that any woman or man's loosed
codes might haunt this grass or get
something like laughed into
the suburbs' outmost lights.
C'mon bloomglutton.
C'mon touchbucket.
I miss the view from where
we waged our little war
on facts and magic—let's head back.
Let's put ourselves roughly
neck-and-neck deep in waived love.

SUR-

One season, the weather went the other way,
and above me, something—an empty trellis?—

appeared so I could snake myself back up it.

That's the way (uh huh, uh huh) I'd like to think
of my having arrived at pain's barricades—

the cursèd place that uncertainty requires—

or of a gift I can neither hold nor have:
permission to prepare to be abandoned.

THE GOOD HISTORIAN

"Blind as light"—three of the right words where wrong ones
would've done—was all I meant then, if not now,
not bound to go the way of louder voices,
many useless as the phrase "the mind itself."
Half enthralled, more peculiar in these mirrors
(not so much as an inch of real skin in 'em!)
I'm ready for birds to warn me to morning,
at which point I'll sleep and know the sun's still there.
I'll know so again beneath the one crushed moon
and in the screensaver's flat glow of jungle.
Almost anything's a toy—I forget that—
and maybe I've moved around the house enough
to've missed the bleached flag expiring on its pole.
I've never closed my mouth to the past; in fact,
I'll cry right now so there's a music in place—
and apropos—of most of what could be here.
I miss dial tones and cigarettes and blizzards;
three earrings hang from staples in a corkboard.
A painting certainly changes, not unlike
the usage of a word I've never spoken—
bit of rain, familiar wind, another room . . .
One thing's for sure, something'll have to go last.
And until then—or, more likely, until well
before then—the usual, saying what I'm

forgetting (soon to be what I've forgotten)
and nostalgia's just the fact of not having
attended to the present in the present.
No rain, a different wind, a failure of room.

You can't not come from nothing, but you can try,
though I don't, and I'd just as soon not think to.

One breeze after another scribbles the field.

Beg for its return—and breath is character,
the single world. There are no "kinds" of living.

POEM WITH A LINE BY

JOHN WHEELWRIGHT

Like culture, nature was for quite some time
its own future, and again, like culture,
it shoved against your very love of it.
But now's the unoriginal elsewhere,
a monument to scraps of nowheres past,
its maintenance the peeling of skins from stones,
a live feed from the center of a blast.

Shrink then to what you wish in space too wide without you
and if in your having been made quite bilious by
some corporate sweets compacted into
cakes for Duchamp's more operable fountains
you've turned your only sail the wrong way,
you're not sorry—yes vacancy—the day
before you like a beach of toppled cairns.

VISAGES

Quietly at times, or else
as loudly as possible, existence
outwits its particulars.

For instance, my reflection's
defective—I'm reversed there,
permanently so,

and so never the "you"
whom everyone hides from me
without trying to—

but in photos, frozen
and in almost no mood,
I look only a little alone.

SLOW SURVIVOR

Everybody told you there'd be days like these—

you hate the grace of the industrial street;
the old outlive the young with some frequency.

Poetry's about the way the world won't look,

and sometimes you worry that the things you hope
that you're afraid of will pass by unnoticed,

you unaware of your own not having flinched,

of there having been nothing to be scared of
in the first place and therefore in the second,

which, when you think of it—which is always—

kind of renders the whole thing senseless, but still . . .
Creation's as savvy as it needs to be.

Beauty can't be bothered with entirety.

˅

It hurts to leave a light on for nobody.

Ditto songs about sad letters, a glass smashed
clean; the song in which those songs were just written.

The mask on something other than your face comes

loose, and what's the story there—or not there—then?
Feeling you've changed without knowing in what way—

time is to body as bootprint is to door—

you force yourself back into the pastoral,
which is itself forced into the summer day.

As of now you could never not have been here,

so let the evening begin in a blaze of doubt,
unless it doesn't, in which case keep plowing

toward whatever you can say you almost are.

FEARFUL DOLL

Not purity the status, but purity the toy,
paraded under clothes thrown over ropes but then

glissading away with the wave of a thought made
celestial so as to be named, its ache

rewound to being just about to happen,
its bitten eyes gone blossom in its brains.

WHY I AM NOT A BUDDHIST

after Charles Bernstein

Time has everything on us
already. You're looking at it.
(We may dispute about stress.)
You're still looking at it.

A day is said to be so many things,
among them the sound of someone
leaving us all alone, a sound that could
but might not slacken into law come spring.

Buried to where marrow will or will
not sleep (and where there's only ever
caving in forever) a core the shape
of what we stand on—pained with sun,

a good spade each—presents
once-vigorous grasses progressing
to dust, the sometimes-loving jet stream
just adjusting what's above us.

Lucid as a wound is the face I make
when of a good mind to parody prayer,
and what with all these goings-on,
tracing the slit in my coffee cup's lid

with my tongue, because, um, "I like it?"
seems not wrong, but delightful. Little
indulgences take the mind off alert
the way a hand might quiet a bell.

POEM FOR A WHILE

How best to rent myself out goes unanswered.
How a story ends is why a story ends.
I often come up with fine plots for stories—
try telling me I've already told you that
and I might pull back in poorly feigned surprise—
but then I forget them because they're not plots,
they're just sad and peculiar scenarios
to which someone more deft could've lent a form.
News of that which never happens travels fast.
Whatever that is, it doesn't not exist.
Why's it me—a connoisseur of sores and mid-
sized fires who blubbers at any old song—
who chokes come time for what we call "narrative,"
be it ornately makeshift or parroted?
Every wave, every other wave, every wave,
every other wave, every thirty-fifth wave—
such is my aesthetic on the PCH,
all up and down one of California's sides,
a fat dark patch of fog tattooed to the sky.
No thunder in the Golden State, no lightning
licking the evening clean back into noontide.
To remake while hating one's being remade
is one of many okay hypocrisies,
and, PM or AM, one o'clock's one chime
never fails to both define and disappoint.

As of the end of the poem in progress,
I will no longer account for anything
that gives me pleasure and threatens no one else.
I guess this means I'd better start trailing off . . .
Afraid of a little pain, are we? We are,
despite the pain's being wholly familiar,
dull as the last in a series of castles.
As sure as a leaf's a brick's antithesis,
the number of nights I'd like a different life
is equal to the number of days I get—
that's the bitterness of being curious.
Nothing I've failed to not know could be nearer.
To be here is to stay put running away.

Not to put too imagined a point on it,
but if I look at this closely, it's a gift,
a largely ridiculous anti-blessing
that makes of everything a cloud of letters
pronounced in the violence between mouth and Earth.
I've no favorite fear of personality,
and there exist just blips of sublimity,
so how could I not've wanted the last light
late in the ash to be a star on the ground,
at least for the durations of my changes?
That some vastness appears to bother with me
isn't manifestly the wrong thing to feel,
though I wonder—is there another hole here
aside from being human and hearing wrong?
The seasons and their unreasonable edicts,
they'll get their own poem soon, the one that goes:

There's nothing it's like to catch sight of you, nor's
there anything it's like to seem to see you.
Unwitting mourners are born every minute.
For pictures from a world I'm the world's fool.
Diving inside me for one new memory,
I love an abyss's inefficiency
and can't do much to inhibit a parade.
Animal or automobile noise or rain—
these mean less than the devices I've tired of,
the sun pushing up just as the power's back.
Freedom from want? Want is all I've almost owned.
I want least want's failure to be words with me.
Mornings I wake to remembering children
and then to waiting for the children themselves.
I wait, too, for any moods to which I'll cloud.
I'd rather smell of detergent than of skin
some mornings—why is that? And when it isn't,
why isn't it? Why can't I just be the same?
Like a dreamt storm of wind survived by most things,
form disappears abruptly at first, as if
form itself were somehow the dream state, and then
gradually, as though the poem were the day.

LOVE POEM

What would pick through our shadows would tear them, too,
were we to give it time enough and reason.

We will, it will—the rest won't be history.
How would you like to go for a walk with me?

I had a friend and he had an apartment.

He refused to put anything on the walls.

I thought this barbaric; he owned a hammer.

I went out and bought him some crutches, some nails.

BROKEN POEM

If a river's like a copy of itself
and no one decides to put an ocean there;
if old stars are torn apart—or rather were—
and the moon's a quality with qualities—
then what? Before I see that my shadow fits,
the part of day when light comes faint and slow
will have its way. I'll see where I was last night,
am now, though that can't matter for much longer.

If there were fires I left without looking back
or thinking—hint: there were—there were others
by which I crouched until they went out, until
the ground on which I started them grew over.
There are times when I think back to either scene—
breathing like I mean it, invented it, know—
a heavy snow having already fallen.

THE NIGHT BEFORE

I QUIT PLAYING MUSIC

I think it was a Tuesday or a Wednesday.
Like a picket fence or an imagined friend,
that evening's weather was sweetly disruptive—
the clouds returning, the river once again
high modernism. I couldn't yet go back—

time was in front of me. I'd managed to step
on an animal—of that I'm quite certain
I was certain—and all the walk home I thought:
[*the clack of the back door lock the clack of the*
back door lock the clack of the back door lock the]

What undid me were days gone invisible,
and that the world—the whole of it facing me—
wouldn't be changed for the worse if I got lost.
I didn't begin my inward squint just then.
I had plans to pluck the works from some machine.

"SUN CRAP IN MY HAND"

Looking up from the flats at nonsense dollars,
I'd like to say that I've cut myself sober
on some sentence's vicarious abuse.
But I don't—I couldn't—so back now to this,
and hope's a mangled airplane in its hangar.
I think I might take your hand into the ground,
and then I think that that might be like being
a thing thick as wind slash good at the ocean.
Grains of body dust, the way we think we sleep—
make believe you me these were made for gauging—
the backs of our lives, two pianos going,
friends and strangers joining forces on a lawn.
Performed against, the sky seems built for evening.
For all I know, the sky was built for evening
or in the hope of some undeafening rest.
Your voice refuses to disguise my bad guess—
and mine's not enough to have frightened us here—
so how is it that we always had children,
that they seem to me more like us than we are?
Occasionally subject to gusts of life,
I push our swing with a crutch, one intestine
of a cloud a small luxury above us,
no proof of this thought's having spidered along.
I forget that my eyes get used to the dark.

I remember how the air felt on a scratch.
And if to rush back into the pain through which
we came's one way to say this, a second way
would be to fail to say anything at all.

PREDATOR VS. PREDATOR

Not that I think that I know better than this:
a new thought falls from wherever its nest was;
the morning's free of season and from hour.

Whatever this is, it works at me for worse.

The earth doesn't do anything in flowers.

SLAVE (JAGGER/RICHARDS)

Darkness's rivets weep white ink, hence the night
sky in a place without much light pollution.
"I'm the one who stands here while you do the work,"
says the one who stands there while you do the work,
who helps the truth to hurt, if that's still doable.

Welcome to a world like everyone else's,
the bottom of a platter of someone's head.
Can't sleep? There's always the question of whether
it's even possible to murder a seed.
On that day in history I wrote these lines—

"prosopagnosia: face blindness (just into
curiosity; dull as evil, I guess)"—
which refused to be a sentence until now.
In my mouth, a song I almost listened to,
a song that used to sound like the future, but

today just suggests the somewhat recent past,
the speed at which I'd be expected to clean
were I able to stain at a different rate.
Too filthy or too pure and I'm no person.
Too filthy or too pure and you're not turned on.

CHARACTER IS LATE

When push comes to tripping over what you've slain,
you won't worry. You're no one anyone knows.

A minute's less sleep and you'd've made that train.
Stand put upon where you are. The doors've closed.

BABEL

The day is perfectly just out of focus.
Its blurred overlay almost fails to pause us.
It's not that we get bored here while we're waiting—
we were bored solid before the beginning—
but there are specific displays of power,
like dropping a word from an off-white tower,
that we hope to call abuses of power
in the future, even if from said tower.

Rain bounces back into itself from the road;
a flag moves, but without our feeling the wind.
The wind moves without our seeing it, and what?
At this point, it's as if we're wearing frameworks
or scaffolds of balsa, crucifixes all,
unaware of what we've been or where we are.
Our doorways don't look out on one another's.
We have our portraits done in charcoal on tar.

THE OLD THING

Position is, of course, where I've ended up—
this house near another one under some trees.
In the sink, a cirrus of blood from a nick;
in the next yard over, a splatter of leaves.

Crimson and. Crimson and. Crimson and. Crimson—
yank the dust or weight the stylus with a coin.
Far factories are busy making apples
made of plastics, all of them equally real.

CREATIVE WRITING

If the classroom is more or less mirrorless,
mirrorful me here's crying his eyes back in
with the shakes of a newly recovered fool.

I teach but two subjects, hello and goodbye,
although everyone already knows hello,
and what could be the lesson plan for goodbye?

A piece of darkness might be called anything—
"failure layer," "ghost forest," "guts on the wind"—
and it's not my place to fling the stars to there.

Now everyone put on your locksmith costumes.
Today's class: how to appear to be helpful;
tonight's: how to mop your way out of the room.

EXCESSIVELY

Tonight I decided I'd quit poetry.
Tonight I heard a mother talk bitterly
to her son, but something in her voice confirmed—
for me if not for you—that the child was loved.
I slept in the moon in a curtainless room.
I heard a fly buzz. I don't know when I died.

Still in airplane mode, devoid of curb appeal,
I have my sanity and its theatrics—
shadows of, shadows from, shadows the whole way
down and/or around the proverbial way
which by itself is just a walked plank of talk
(most of it level if you can believe that)—
to re-convince myself that all is not speed,
although I might digest creatures with faces,
play tennis without anything forever.

I don't remember you ever touching me.
I was touchable of course, very much so,
but that's got nothing to do with memory.
The jobs this American will do include
spilling syllables from the aggravated
slash I call a mouth out back of dark houses
and picking up heaven, holding it all there
forever—I do these, and you do them too.
"*Seems* to disappear"? What is it that you see?
I don't remember me ever touching you.

POEM BEGINNING WITH A

LINE BY GRANT MCLENNAN

A white moon appears like a hole in the sky,
I repeat, reply, the rain here not seeming
to matter, the dark the very blue I'd try—
as when a singer knows where to put her voice—
to hallucinate were it not wholly real.
The front of this week's *New Yorker* is clever
about catastrophe: them's the references.
I know them and I won't have them sold to me.
Selectively restless, admittedly starred,
I—as when someone should speak of pasturing
bees—was wrong: the heart is dirt; several bells sound
new as they explode into less than pieces.
They tell us there's more than one time. Why do that?
But I'd hate them, right, if they didn't do that?

POEM TO MY SON

"How am I for time?" seems the only question,
the only promising reply, "All for it."
Before dawn I woke to gray maples, the sun
just up over somewhere I thought I could live,
and I answered your question about God
dishonestly, for fear that my lack of faith
would somehow dissuade you from faith generally,
thus obliterating my sense of duty.
(To tell the truth later will be selfish too,
but I wore through the afternoon anyway.)
Now, day's lost; the night's inched back from its hiding;
and at the edge of whatever I look like,
look: no anything, no poem, no dying.
"Edgar Poe wanted the fool in *Lear* to fly

a black kite," writes Norman Dubie, as do I
(as in "I want that as well" and "I typed it"),
but what good advices can I hand to you
given your place in the new next world? The dark
we inhabit is neither fabric nor stain—
what I'm always saying, whatever I say—
and other things click true: a downpour's stronger
when you're standing still; knowing full well just how
contorted the mind is, we've all been floored by

"If I believe in X, then why not in Y?";
and even if you imagine otherwise,
you'd go back in time if that were possible,
as life stays mostly quiet in its blindspots.
All there is is that some parts of it might not.

NIGHT YEARS

I close an eye and then thumb out a streetlight.

It's not the best vandalism, but it's mine.

TO THE SPEAKER

Made you—look!—but I'm leaving; you can have you.
Here's nothing I couldn't've anticipated:
95 messages, 93 unread;

stacks of damp dollars on the bar all summer;
two clouds over there, their playfully blatant
failures to be water, both neutral as gold.

To hear screams and wish you had a camera;
to've been served a small salad by a goth kid.
You could go on, did in fact go on like that

in "Real Job," a poem a patient stranger,
a student of a poet I've never met,
once memorized and maybe still calls to mind.

Made, you look—and I'm leaving so you'll see it.
You stay here for someone; I'll head home alone.
That moon is not so bright as to burn the eyes.

"A little quiet and it all comes apart"
could be a sentence in which "it" means "quiet."
If our mirrors break alike, this poem dies.

ROLL OVER

The good days in something other than a row—
movement without progress, anyone's shadow—

I tend to speak *in* sentences, not *with* them,
but it's not my fault that they feel like places—

or rather, it's not my fault that it's my fault
that I might live beyond this untried face.

Calling the inability to forget
"memory" is like calling a bruised leaf "Dave."

Listen here: this "is," I fumble it toward you.
You can have it all if you play persuaded.

WHITMANIC

If the lazy hum of drones in leaves of grass
is any indication of anything,
it's not the summer, but my ability
to still recall the ranks and noises of bees,
the "lately buzzing" of those in *Leaves of Grass*.
My greed is such that when a WALK sign offers
up the chance to travel blocks out of my way,
I, the kind kind of colonist, drop bread crumbs.
I'm framed by the day the way a boat is framed
by a lake: a little unforgivingly;
both pleased and panicked by my being almost
always closer to one end or the other,
the day's exact center being hard to suss,
I take my vistas from a flag full of holes.

Sun's insistence, the low notes of a copter—
these are somehow as if without precedent,
like forgetting how to play an instrument
or the qualities of the newly unborn.
If I can't bring myself to want to love it
then it interests me, as in my new pursuit
called "evening" coming on like a cartoon shroud
or the kinglet whistling loud behind that house.
Nothing's just another word for not having
the freedom to throw my shit into the street

or for what I'd hope would be beneath these boots
had I time and half a mind to look for it.
America's what I assume it to be,
and yet, as ever, or more often than that,
disquiet pulls its plow through every part of me.

CREEPS

Time swims, and mind edges out its environs.
I imagine and unimagine myself—

another day, the way the sun makes things feel,
the way the point seems once I've failed to see it.

Once, on an airplane, I had my key ring swiped.
I was sleeping, flying away from my car.

I want to love everyone more than I do.
I want to love everyone more than you do.

Shown a film of something I've done, I might not
or might want to do that thing a second time.

MEAT AND READER

Fables of meat've always meant the same thing.
Actual people often wander through them.
They go singing in their only direction,
their notes and words disappearing through their mouths
the way an ocean gets darker farther out.
Dreamt to here by whatever priority,
what's called a world films them, and that's what they'll be.
Sometimes affirmed as beyond its own debris,
the inevitable's quote not having it
unquote, its halo now bent into a frame.
I get the feeling you've heard this one before,
because you will have by the time it's over.

Reader, I marry you—this is how it's done—
and when I have fears that I have no business
messing with an additional paradise,
that "God" is the inkling that there's not much else,
I can't make sense without breaking my pencil.
There's no asking the sky to do anything,
as that would be to misunderstand magic
(or at least its role in what's left of what is).
You could, as they say, get a rise out of me,
beat the being-out-of-context out of me.
I could get used to my getting used all day.
All poetry's dead animal poetry.

AGGRESSIVELY MINOR

Flowers've been around approximately
one billion five hundred sixty million months—
most of these before the month was invented—
and unlike me, they know just when they're to die.
He who expires with the brightest detritus
glints now and again from a stone or a screen,
and of course the same thing's true for the ladies.
If on some days I have the worst taste in light
(and if on those days life still seems possible)
on others living lacks a definition,
and what are *you* going to do about it,
italics mine because they make it sound right,
poetry being an oral art and all.
There's always the sad fiction of not wanting
whatever it is one needs, but let's just say
that that's what's called "a living"—is that okay?
Joy's not an oil poured on everyone at once,
but most of us get some sooner than never.
Spring's of course been a postscript to the winter—
the bad news bad, the good of no consequence,
my body almost forgotten in itself.
Dumb questions might be better than their answers,
which is reason enough for staying alive.
Why won't I title this poem something else,
and what would one day without peril be like?

Well I'll be damned—and damned well for the most part:
there's not really a future tense in English;
David Geffen's sale of Jasper Johns' *False Start*
(from which I got several of my ideas)
got Geffen eighty million bucks in '06;
and I write this poem in Honolulu!
My own stuff sleeps easy in its worthlessness.
My words construe my use, but what does "I" do?

"Something" might well be the past tense of "nothing,"
and "pluck" is just the thing that lacks those feathers
I had hoped were little flames out on the waves.
A trance one knows one's in defeats its purpose
(or does it?), but that's literature for us.
One's weather mind put out, "I" works like a curse.

NIGHT YEARS

Asleep, I'm not the only thing about me.

My shirt's extra buttons are cold on my rib;
the swollen river makes a noise like chewing.

I'm somewhere, but I can't say just where that is.

To try to say is said to bore the listener,
who has more inconsequential things to do.

VICARIOUS

Before they were born—I shrink to admit this—
whenever I thought of my kids getting sick
or being injured or dying, I thought mostly
of the chances of my going to prison.
Now they're in front of me, running through some waves,
and what I am is all but buoyant with pain.

EARLY BLIZZARD

after Stevens

Morning destroys the old future all morning—
entirely, as one might elect to attack a large pill.

I'll always have time for the gods and the dead;
that said, that's what I said, I who—not quite dead

and not myself a god—pretend to stare at the cold
red water of some half-forsaken river I've invented.

A cashed nickel bag sticks to the light-rail tracks,
and many, many weightless white flakes've cracked a branch.

Hours at a time, a wanting cynosure, me,
my face if it were printed on money (I mean it),

I turn away and talk the whole time time breaks me in,
and this was only the only new year of my life—

the same wind twice and twice the letting go,
October snow on a parked public-works truck.

Back when you could drink from a river without getting sick,
I wasn't there yet, nor am I now in this wet rush inside a thirst.

SOUL MAN

Not again . . . Before no God and nobody
my stanza advances discourageably;
my skin's the wall between the things I call "me";
and if at first I don't believe I succeed,
I look exactly like what I can carry.
Body, the; city, the; economy, the—
there's no disaster like this middle classing,
my trying to jerk a word into the day.
(Got what I got the odd way: wrote some poems
and some people gave me some money for 'em,
though they're still mine for whatever that's not worth.)
Surrounded by downtown's ghostly social skills,
I'd like to tear history a new angel
from one of those phone books I no longer use,
and if no one wants it then that's what happens—
I make no move to move out of the index.
Here, and worriedly cupping a cloudy eye,
I understand I need my little fear box.

SELF-PORTRAIT IN

A BOTTLE OF NYQUIL

The sweet wood of houses has nothing on skin.
That I'll owe myself to sleep is for certain.
Forever over there, beginning never,
the stars are great strangers, the sun tears the air,
the heart of all time is I'm being pulled down.

The heart of being is I'm being forced out,
and while I know it as all that might be real,
this earth's the false bottom of its universe.
(I could swear the wind is propping up these walls.)

Night years, layers of glass, the invisible,
the risible, the possible, the palsied.
There's a difference between never having heard
a sound and having heard a sound a hundred
thousand times before failing to recall it.

There are ways of making me talk and then look.
There are ways of making me the President.
A mirror's not throat or mouth to anything,
but when it tries to get its word in, I fit.

Noisy idea I neither get nor lose,
I don't choose between an ashtray and a bowl.
Astride the point, thinking's lovely and empty.
If time's a chrysanthemum, space is a hole.

WILD KINGDOM

Flies haul bits of shit into the fruited air
for real. They don't seem to mean to, but they do.

In alcohol years, it's your birthday somewhere.
You smell like a person. You act like one too.

WOULD

Little use in touching it, no use in not—
the sunken nailhead of a word that you said
and wanted more than anything to yank back.

INCREMENTAL

for Elisa Gabbert

Lived and living, between which I grow my way,
a way from which, as from facts, I tend to stray
by rising easily into disrepair;
by vanishing into countless nervous moves.
When that's not possible—though it always is—
I look to mountains to get at what's past them;
I sit by an ocean to see where it goes.

While waiting for sleep's good creases to my face,
I think—but also brace for dreams of lesions;
I do what I can to sink after the sun,
which would mean to go where *it* goes, but later,
while waiting for sleep's good creases to my face,
I think—but also brace—for dreams of lesions.
I do what I can to sink after the sun,
which would mean to go where *it* goes, but later.

EVERYONE'S JUVENILIA

It's not as if everyone's not in this life.
It's as if there sits a sky below the world.

Only two squares left on the tired year's grid,
two days until toasts to the negligible.

A portable restroom tumbling down a road—
and on YouTube of all the glowing so-called

places I suddenly find myself at night
when I should be reading or sleeping or dead—

is no tumbleweed, though it's just as useful
as any clicked-on and laughed-into-shape thing.

Too late to be what I might've been? I'll say.
Everyone's his or her own juvenilia

and everything's evidence—to fault oneself
for having been someone else is fruitless pain.

We can't help the fiction that we're in each day.
We're in each day in the same way we're in flames.

POEM

Stay, illusion! —HORATIO

You, shadow I could name after nothing,
silent inside some circuitry's breathing,
you don't see me, but I'm what seems to be
biting my way through April's clamped blossoms,
a busted alarm for lack of vespers,
better things to do for lack of a cause.
I yield back the balance of my safety,
gladly, unless it's all gone, in which case
I yield back my monopoly on me.
Splintered water—not ice, but fractured drops
if that's possible, which it seems to be—
there's that word again, "seems": I don't know it
or know it only in my ignorance,
so where was I? Of course: splintered water—
not ice, but fractured drops—each could in time
become a lens through which you might catch me,
though they can't yet be fashioned for such use,
however pictured they may come to be
or not be in the blindness between us.
Through one or many more faults of my own,
notions to which I might've clung collapse
and I would call that the end of the sound
of thoughts arriving from another mind

only to return to their own nowhere
as strained and as disabled as they came.
There comes a time when one is far too young
to be answerable to anyone,
but this can't be the case for very long.
About the rain, I was given the wrong
information, but not about the song
about the rally to a yearly low
that would erase us back to nature.
Much later, comma, illusory stone,
rooms of it, some feeling in its debris
wished out, and yet this isn't how it sounds:
another branch from which to pull lemons,
another reason not to chrome the moon.
I live with you barely in front of me,
and patience is another kind of time,
but if for better or less than okay
today won't outlive itself by a day,
don't cry—besides, tatters can be pretty,
and in the near midst of its losing me
my mind wants memory, not history,
history having been drained of excess
or maybe filled with excess's opposite:
you, shadow, outgoingly unholy,
whom I now name after nothing but this.

ACKNOWLEDGMENTS

I'm grateful to the editors of the following journals and websites, where versions of these poems first appeared: The Academy of American Poets' "Poem-A-Day" series, *Better*, *Boston Review*, *Cannibal*, *Chicago Quarterly Review*, *Conduit*, *Court Green*, *The Cultural Society*, *Fence*, *Gulf Coast*, *jubilat*, *Lo-Ball*, *Noö Weekly*, *Notre Dame Review*, *The Pinch*, *Poor Claudia*, *A Public Space*, *Smoking Glue Gun*, *Typo*, *The Volta*, *The White Review*, and *Witness*. "Visages" first appeared in *Privacy Policy: The Anthology of Surveillance Poetics*, edited by Andrew Ridker (Black Ocean, 2014). Thanks to Wolfram Swets, "Time Down to Mind" and "Night Years ('I close an eye . . .')" were printed as letterpress postcards by Tungsten Press. Thanks to Sean Patrick Hill, "Let This Be the Poem for a Face I Almost Made" was printed as a letterpress broadside by Green Fuse Press.

Born in Tennessee and raised in Wisconsin, Graham Foust is the author of five previous books of poems, including *To Anacreon in Heaven and Other Poems* (Flood Editions, 2013), a finalist for the Believer Poetry Award. With Samuel Frederick, he has also translated three books by the late German poet Ernst Meister, including *Of Entirety Say the Sentence* (Wave Books, 2015). He works at the University of Denver.